Scientists at Work

by Susan Ring

Consultant: Brian VanVoorst, Principal Research Scientist,
Honeywell Labs

Yellow
Umbrella
Books
for early readers

Yellow Umbrella Books are published by Red Brick Learning
7825 Telegraph Road, Bloomington, Minnesota 55438
http://www.redbricklearning.com

Editorial Director: Mary Lindeen
Senior Editor: Hollie J. Endres
Photo Researcher: Signature Design
Developer: Raindrop Publishing
Consultant: Brian VanVoorst, Principal Research Scientist, Honeywell Labs
Conversion Assistants: Jenny Marks, Laura Manthe

Library of Congress Cataloging-in-Publication Data
Ring, Susan
  Scientists at work / by Susan Ring
    p. cm.
  ISBN 0-7368-5837-7 (hardcover)
  ISBN 0-7368-5267-0 (softcover)
  1. Science—Vocational guidance—Juvenile literature. 2. Scientists--Juvenile literature. I. Title.
  Q147.R56 2005
  502.3—dc22

                                    2005015659

Photo Credits:
Cover: Gary Braasch/ZUMA Press; Title Page: Jupiter Images; Page 2: Ed Lallo/Index Stock
Imagery; Page 3: Sean Gallup/Getty Images, Inc.; Page 4: Joe Koshollek/KRT; Page 5: Pierre
Vauthey/Corbis Sygma; Page 6: Les Stone/ZUMA Press; Page 7: Corbis; Page 8: Paola Andrea
Martinez/Notimex; Page 9: Aladin Abdel Naby/Reuters Photo Archive; Page 10: NASA
PHOTO/Agence France Presse; Page 11: Getty Images/Getty Images, Inc.; Page 12: Yuriko
Nakao/Reuters Photo Archive; Page 13: Deutsch Presse Agentur; Page 14: Gary
Braasch/ZUMA Press

1 2 3 4 5 6 11 10 09 08 07 06

Table of Contents

Many Kinds of Scientists

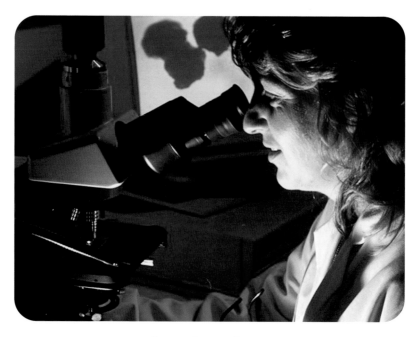

There are many kinds of scientists. They all work to understand our world better. Scientists use different kinds of tools. This scientist is using a **microscope**. She is looking at germs that can make people sick.

This scientist is working to discover a new kind of medicine. He is working in a **lab**. Other scientists sometimes work in very unusual places. Let's take a look at some other scientists at work.

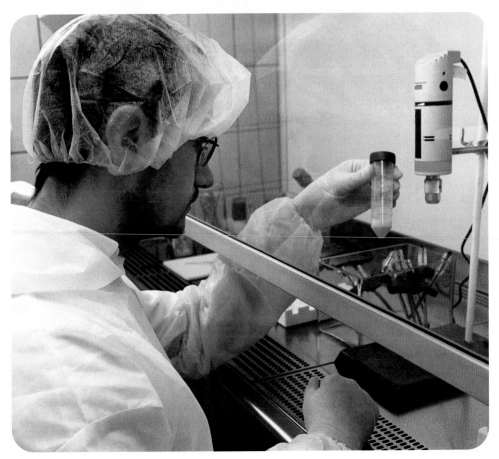

In the Wild

These scientists work outdoors. Their job is to study wild animals. They can't make the animals come to them, so they go where the animals are.

These scientists are studying bears. They want to know more about why bears **hibernate**.

This scientist studies plants. These plants are in a rain forest. Scientists know that the plants here can help people. Some plants can be a source of medicine. Every day, scientists discover new things.

Under the Sea

This scientist also works outdoors. Much of her work takes place in the ocean. She is studying dolphins. She wants to learn as much as she can about these sea creatures. Like all scientists, she asks questions and looks for answers.

This scientist also works under the sea. She is looking at a **coral reef**. The reef is full of life. The scientist wants to make sure that the reef is healthy. She is taking pictures. She will study them when she is back on land.

Digging Up the Past

These scientists are digging for **fossils**. They study what life was like millions of years ago. Here they have found some dinosaur bones! When the scientists are finished studying the bones, they might send them to a museum.

This scientist is also studying the past. He is looking at a mummy. He also looks at things that were buried with the mummy. Each little object gives him clues about the past.

Out in Space

This scientist is performing experiments in space. He is on a **space station**. He will stay up in space for a few months. Like all scientists, he has studied hard to learn his job.

These scientists study space, too. They watch a rover move on Mars. The rover is like a robot. It takes pictures and sends them back to Earth. These scientists know how to study the photos and what to look for in each one.

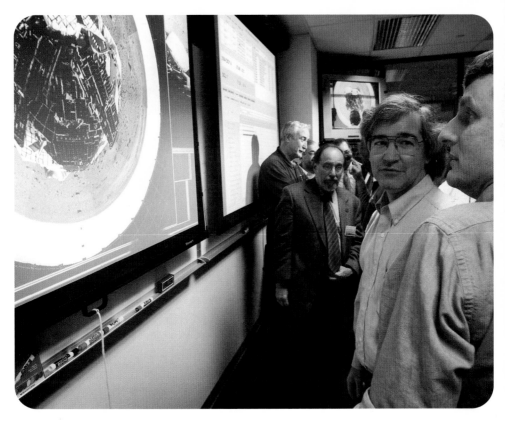

On the Move

Here is another type of robot on the move! These scientists build robots. The robots will be able to go places and do some of the same things that people can. It takes a long time to build robots.

These scientists are working on making a better car. What will the cars of the future look like? Like all scientists, these scientists must **experiment** before they get exactly what they want.

From high up in space to deep under the sea, scientists study all sorts of things. There are many kinds of scientists. If you were to become a scientist, what would you study?

Glossary

coral reef—a collection of very small animals living together to form a rock-like structure under the ocean

experiment—a test that is set up to answer a question

fossils—pieces of bone or other once-living things that have turned to stone

hibernate—to go to sleep for the whole winter

lab—a room with special equipment where scientists do experiments

microscope—a tool that lets people see tiny objects

space station—a research center in space where people live and work for long periods of time

Index

Word Count: 483
Early-Intervention Level: M